# mountain bike madness

## j. p. partland
## john gibson

MBI

**To my family for indulging and supporting my interests.
To that guy who loaned me his mountain bike in 1985.
And to Beth for finding dirty ears amusing.**
*—J. P. Partland*

**I thank my parents for their encouragement, along with Jake Heilbron,
Richard Cox, and Derek Westerlund. I thank Jean for everything else.**
*—John Gibson*

This edition first published in 2003 by
MBI Publishing Company, Galtier Plaza,
Suite 200, 380 Jackson Street, St. Paul, MN
55101-3885 USA

MBI Publishing Company titles are also available
at discounts in bulk quantity for industrial or
sales-promotional use. For details write to Special
Sales Manager at Motorbooks International
Wholesalers & Distributors, Galtier Plaza, Suite 200,
380 Jackson Street, St. Paul, MN 55101-3885 USA.

Library of Congress Cataloging-in-Publication
Data Available
ISBN 0-7603-1440-3

## About the Authors

J.P. Partland first swung his leg over a bicycle when
he was three. Little did he know it would become
a lifelong obsession. An avid biker, his work has
appeared on numerous Web sites and in more than
fifty cycling-specific and general interest magazines,
including *Velo News, Asphalt, Bicycling, Bicyclist,
Bike, Women's Sports and Fitness, Fitness, Hooked
on the Outdoors,* and *Outside.* In addition to his
work as a journalist, he has also performed stand-
up comedy, and written plays, teleplays, and short
stories. He still finds there is never enough time to
ride and never enough room for bikes. Mr. Partland
lives in New York City.

John Gibson spent the first ten years of his
photography career as a newspaper photographer
in Calgary, Alberta, Canada. In 1996, he started
photographing the mountain bike scene and
immersed himself in the bicycle industry. Now, he
travels the world taking pictures of people riding
their bikes. When he's not shooting pictures, he
enjoys riding the trails that start right outside his
home. Mr. Gibson lives in the Canadian Rocky
Mountains in the province of Alberta.

All photos by John Gibson, except where indicated.

Edited by Chad Caruthers
Designed by LeAnn Kuhlmann

Printed in China

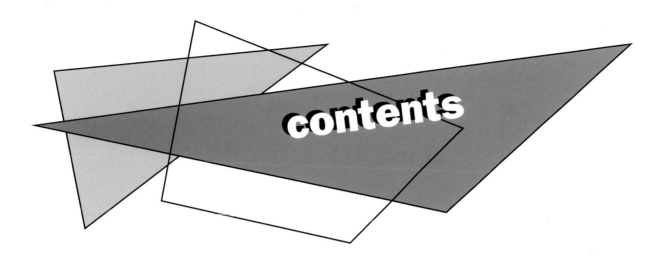

# contents

# acknowledgments

**There are many people** to thank for their help on this book. Most of the people mentioned or quoted aren't remote figures but are real folks who are still riding their bikes and working jobs and took the time to answer my questions. I tip my helmet to all those who patiently answered my lengthy queries. Two I'd like to mention by name are Don Cook of the Mountain Bike Hall of Fame, who helped track down countless phone numbers, and Joe Breeze, who has a serious interest in making sure that myth doesn't usurp fact.

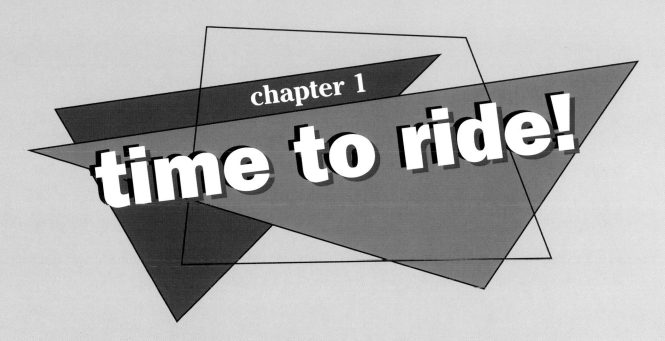

# time to ride!

## the roots of mountain biking

**Not so long ago,** a bicycle was born. In a far-western county named Marin, on a mountain called Tam, some enlightened folks brought forth the mountain bike. Three hippie hedonist free spirits were pushing their old bikes to the top of the mountain to bomb down it. These bikes were heavy, one-speed, coaster-brake deals that most people would be embarrassed to own, let alone ride. The bikes were known as "cruisers" or "newsboys"—sometimes known by the Schwinn model Black Phantom—bikes that first appeared in the 1930s and were fueled by the popularity of cars and motorcycles. These old steeds were the antithesis of the skinny-tired, drop-handlebar road racers that had taken the country by storm during the oil crisis of the 1970s.

Riders take a break on Mt. Tam, which is regarded as the birthplace of mountain biking.

Appearances didn't matter to this band of thrill-seeking souls. They wore heavy boots and layers of thick clothing to protect them if they biffed. Danger? The rush was worth it. The ride was the embodiment of freedom. It was like they were kids again in the woods behind their house. Only their moms weren't going to complain if they came home muddied and scraped up.

*Danger?*
*The rush was worth it.*
*The ride was the embodiment*
*of freedom.*

They told a few friends, their friends told a few friends, and before you could say "Eddy Merckx," they had an event. The Repack was the ride, because they'd have to repack their ancient coaster brake hubs after each run. They'd have to repack because the heat generated by employing the brake overheated the hub to the point that the grease liquidized and ran out of the hub.

Repacking was the least of it. Finding bikes suitable for the task was *really* difficult. Most of the coolest frames were old and rare and so unappreciated that even junkyards weren't taking them. Replacement parts were hard to find. Breakage was common, so available stock was running out fast. This gang was not familiar with limits, so it learned how to weld to fix broken frames. Then, these bikers started improving frames before they broke. Next, somebody added a rear derailleur and a five-speed freewheel. Presto! The bike could go uphill as well as down.

The junk supply was almost gone, so somebody went out and built a frame just for the task. It was such a good idea; every member of the Repack gang wanted one. So the bikes were built and bought. These new bikes were lighter and didn't have to be overhauled after each run.

Word began to spread. Whispers reached beyond Marin County, California, to other parts of the Bay Area. The bike was aggro. The bike was cool. Maybe everyone would want one. Somebody in a CBS office in San Francisco heard about these hippies and wanted to shoot these riders. In 1979, *CBS Evening News* did a segment on this new phenomenon.

Specialized Bicycle Components introduced the Stumpjumper in the fall of 1981. Amazingly, everyone wanted one. The revolution had begun. These "mountain" bikes sold like hotcakes, so every manufacturer had to build one. Bike component makers created new parts to replace the motorcycle parts. The bike got lighter and faster. The World Championship took place in 1990, in Colorado, less than a decade after the first mountain bike was mass-produced. The winners were Americans. The revolution was over. The world would never be the same.

### Mountain Bike Myth, Mountain Bike Reality

Mt. Tam's full name is Mount Tamalpais. It sits in the middle of Marin County, across the Golden Gate Bridge from San Francisco. Many of mountain biking's pioneers came from towns surrounding Mt. Tam.

Some people say that the three wisemen at the beginning were Gary Fisher, Tom Ritchey, and Charles Kelly. Not a bad hypothesis, as the trio formed a joint venture in 1979, the year Ritchey first showed up at the Repack. The business was MountainBikes. It began with Ritchey building three bikes: one for himself, one for Fisher, and one for sale.

Gary Fisher, one of the founders of the mountain bike, with his 29-inch prototype wheel and bike that was designed to use 29-inch wheels. A standard mountain bike wheel is 26 inches. Fisher brought this bike to race in the master's division at the 2000 Napa World Cup in California.

The problem with this hypothesis is that the Repack is a bit older. The first Repack race was organized in 1976, and it was on Pine Mountain, not on Mt. Tam. Ritchey didn't make his first appearance at The Repack until 1979.

In addition, mountain biking was going on well before The Repack began. Others say Joe Breeze, Otis Guy, and Marc Vendetti were the first three—another reasonable guess, as the first two also went on to build bikes. The threesome first rode up (no pushing—they never pushed) the mountain-access road to

bomb the trail descent in 1973. They were locals to the area, and Vendetti, a motorcyclist turned cyclist, had convinced the other two it would be fun. He even pushed Breeze to buy his first Schwinn Excelsior for $5 at a junkyard in Santa Cruz.

Vendetti, however, had already been doing this for some time. He had gotten into it with friends from his hometown of Larkspur, just north of Mt. Tam and west of Fairfax, where Breeze lived. The Larkspur gang had probably been riding since 1970 or earlier.

> ## *Saying that mountain biking began at Mt. Tam isn't fair to all the other folks who were doing it in other places.*

Saying that mountain biking began at Mt. Tam isn't fair to all the other folks who were doing it in other places. Some say it was the Morrow Dirt Club, in Cupertino, California. The club's ten members would meet weekly to ride the fire roads around Cupertino. This was back in 1974. Significantly, one of the Morrow gang, Russ Mahon, had put derailleurs on his old cruiser so he could expand his riding reach.

As well, the Morrow Dirt Club isn't the only group with a claim. There was a Colorado "Klunker Tour" from Crested Butte to Aspen in the fall of 1976. The local newspaper, the *Crested Butte Pilot,* covered the event. It stands to reason that these cyclists were riding off-road some time before the event transpired.

While the East Coast scene isn't as storied, there are reports of cyclists taking cyclocross bikes into the woods of Massachusetts, New Hampshire, and Pennsylvania in the 1970s. There was a club called The Bombers in State College, Pennsylvania, a club whose rules for admission included that

Pioneers Owen Mullholland, Joe Breeze, Otis Guy, and Boyd Watkins at Pikes Peak, in Colorado. Breeze is riding a Breezer of his own design and construction, while Guy is on an Otis Guy, designed and built himself. *Photo by David Epperson*

Bikers, including Joe Breeze (fourth from right) and Otis Guy (third from right), take a break. Note the designs and characteristics of these early bikes. *Photo by David Epperson*

the bike had to weigh at least 50 pounds and cost less than $100.

Shortly after Ritchey's first mountain bikes started leaving the Bay Area, Chris Chance, Gary Helfrich, and John Troja started building Fat Chance bikes in Massachusetts. They differed from their West Coast brethren, as they were adapted to the steep, narrow, and rocky trails that are more common in the East.

In most cases, the guys who are credited with inventing the mountain bike had considerable road bike experience. Many of them were racing road bikes, even if they did look like stereotypical "dope-smoking hippies." A number of them were very good riders who competed among the best of the United States. Some were racing a niche discipline called cyclocross. Some were building road bikes. While they were trudging up Mt. Tam with their one-speed cruisers, they were also riding their road and 'cross bikes in the woods. Tom Ritchey, while not really from the Mt. Tam gang, was a former top junior racer. Ritchey had decided that frame building was the trade he wanted to practice, and he had been building road bikes for several years before he teamed up with Gary Fisher and Charles Kelly to form MountainBikes in 1979.

Before the MountainBikes venture, Joe Breeze had built several mountain bikes. He was building road frames already, so the know-how was there. Breeze built ten mountain bikes in 1977 and 1978. The Breezer was purpose-built for mountain biking—lighter and stronger than the old cantilevered frameset that had become the standard.

Around the time of the early Breezers, Mert Lawill was trying to sell Pro Cruisers up and down California. He had built 500 of these early mountain bikes and was going from dealer to dealer trying to convince shop owners that this overgrown BMX bike had a future. They seemed to sell better in Southern California.

In 1979, a portion of the Marin gang went to Crested Butte to try the Pearl Pass Tour. This meeting increased communications and sped evolution. A young member of the Crested Butte, Colorado crowd, Don Cook, started spending time in Marin every year to soak up knowledge and bring it home.

When Specialized came out with the Stumpjumper in 1981, Univega came out with the Alpina Pro. It was designed by James McLean, who's given credit for coining the term *mountain bike*. The term quickly gained currency over "klunker."

Back then, Specialized was a smallish national brand that was selling high-end bike stuff. The company had connections to Italy and Japan. They were often getting things made or labeled overseas and bringing them to the United States for sale. They started the Stumpjumper line with 125 frames designed in the United States and built in Japan, and put the parts kits together in California. Specialized chief Mike Sinyard bet his salespeople that they couldn't sell the initial shipment in a month. They sold out in six days, and more were back-ordered. Then, 5 more containers arrived and more back orders. Then 10 more.

Specialized's marketing director, Rick Vosper, who back then was one of the company's two salespeople, saw the moment as one of convergence. "I think the mountain bike boom in general and the Stumpjumper in particular was one of those planets-in-alignment things where nothing happens at all until all the elements are in place, and then everything happens at once." Specialized, unlike Pro Cruiser, MountainBikes, and Univega, had a very well-established sales network across the country and could get bikes into shops as well as spread the word.

## The Madness of the Myth

Creation myths are easy to believe. They explain everything in a nice bundle. The truth is, there isn't really a single beginning to mountain biking. Many people were doing many similar things at the same time. The idea caught on, and communication then sped the process of evolution.

Off-road riding really began with the creation of the bicycle. Most roads in the nineteenth century were similar to jeep tracks of today. The ordinary penny-farthing high wheel was one response to the rough roads. The huge front wheel rolled easily over uneven and rutted roads.

What really started the bike revolution, though, was the pneumatic tire. Scot John Dunlop's pneumatic tire, patented in 1888, was

Joe Breeze followed by Otis Guy near the end of the 1984 Pearl Pass Tour in Crested Butte, Colorado. *Photo by David Epperson*

a huge step forward for bikes. The air-filled tire made bicycles with chain drives and identically sized front and rear wheels a winning bike design. By the end of the 1890s, bikes were everywhere, a fad of incredible proportion, one that changed the physical and cultural land-scape of its era. Peter Nye, a cycling historian, explained those days. "At the turn of the twen-tieth century, the United States had less than 150 miles of paved roads, chiefly in urban areas. Manufactured goods were sent long distances from manufacturer to market by train." With such a lack of paved roads, and the obvious fact that more would make cycling easier, more practical, and even more popular, the League of American Wheelmen, a bike lobby, pushed for additional paved roads throughout the country.

The famed Buffalo Soldiers rode bicycles around the West as an experiment in 1896. Some might say they were the original moun-tain bikers.

## The truth is, there isn't really a single beginning to mountain biking.

The cruiser bike, which debuted in 1933, became the most obvious parent of the mountain bike and was a departure from the norm in its time. The air-filled "balloon" tires were unusual in the United States and were a hit, according to Jay Pridmore and Jim Hurd in their book, *The American Bicycle*. The cruiser bike was built for comfort and durability, and it held true to form. The cruiser, however, with its one gear and coaster brake, was essentially capable of only riding slowly on flat roads. Some folks called them "newsboys," because it was the kind of bike one might see a paperboy riding. The big tires were slow on pavement, and the upright position of the rider was about as un-aerodynamic as it could get. Possibly one of the cruiser's biggest curses was that it was sold as a kid's toy and not as a viable mode of adult transportation. When the cruiser came about, drop-handlebar racing bikes with narrow tires already existed. Also around this time, geared bikes were starting to dot the European bike scene.

Cruisers were often gussied up to be as motorcycle-like as possible—a motorless motorcycle for kids, a toy. Huge chrome fenders, fat whitewall tires, large fake gas tanks, a mega seat, and a heavy rack were often standard accessories. Sometimes these bikes were wired for lights and a radio.

When the cruisers found a way out of junkyards as early klunkers, they needed serious work before being deemed dirtworthy. In order to convert the cruisers for off-road use, the bikes were stripped down to the bone. Everything that wasn't necessary was removed. This would convert a 65-pound beast into an almost-svelte 40-pound descending machine.

When the brakes proved to be a limitation, the early mountain bikers realized that brakes designed for touring and cyclocross bikes would provide better stopping power at a cost of less weight. Cantilever studs were brazed on and canti' brakes were mounted. One problem solved.

When the frames broke, the early riders looked to modern frame tubes and the latest in brazing technology. The original bike parts were usually heavy and made of stamped steel. These parts were replaced by lightweight cold-forged parts. Touring bikes had been taking advantage of a wide range of gears, so touring parts were put onto the bikes to handle pedaling

A rider takes on the trails of Crested Butte, Colorado, astride a bike by Otis Guy. *Photo by David Epperson*

up and down the steepest inclines. Since the riders were used to fast-handling road bikes, designers shied away from the slack geometry favored by cruisers so that the bikes would handle faster.

The important thing is that people were always riding bikes off-road. The various currents floating around different parts of the country started to converge into small groups in a number of places. When word of the off-road riding groups started spreading to other off-road groups, there was a realization that this was a trend. Momentum gathered and someone was bound to try something that would succeed. Journalists and businesses spread the word around the country, and suddenly the new thrill was the next big thing.

As the new mountain bike gained in popularity, more bike manufacturers built them. Component manufacturers designed specific parts, and tire makers designed new treads. In a few years, mountain bike parts that had been borrowed from both motorcycles and touring bikes largely disappeared.

A new type of bike had been born.

The lush greenery of the hillside trails on Mt. Tam offer the perfect backdrop for riding. The sad irony is that most of the singletrack trails on Mt. Tam are now closed to mountain bike riding.

# chapter 2
# no-tech to high-tech

## the ride evolves

**The mountain bike,** known and loved around the world for its rough-hewn, confidence-inspiring good looks, rose like a phoenix from the ashes of the fallen cruiser. Over the years, a combination of broken parts, design genius, garage tinkering, rider preference, manufacturing needs, cost limitations, and luck transformed that mountain bike into what it is today.

### Klunkers
The klunker, properly spelled with a "k" and not a "c," was certainly onomato-poetic. It looked and rode like something respectable cyclists didn't want to own. For many of the early aficionados, this aesthetic was deliberate. They idealized the anti-bike: simple, heavy, slow, castoff, in need of fresh paint. These bikes represented the color of the sport.

Joe Schwartz of the Kona Clump FreeRide Team makes good use of his disc brakes on a film shoot in Morocco.

Of course, the intended use of klunkers capitalized on all their drawbacks. Simple design minimized maintenance and mechanical failures. Heavy parts survived rough conditions and high-speed crashes. Despite the fact that they were slow on pavement, klunkers handled well in the dirt. Their cast-off look added to their character and was due to the fact that new parts weren't made for these ancient steeds. And because riding was sufficiently harsh, new stuff got old quickly.

*Despite the fact that they were slow on pavement, klunkers handled well in the dirt. Their cast-off look added to their character.*

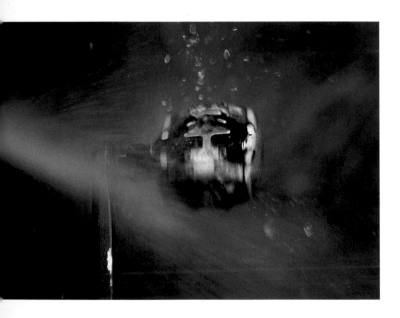

This is a first-generation SPD pedal, which has since been replaced with a smaller and lighter version.

Once seen as an end, a hoot, a bike that no one cared about, each klunker found a place in the heart of its owner. Eventually, they became cherished, and ultimately they could klunk no more. A custom bike could do the job better. "Better" included lighter, more durable, more gears, better brakes, and better tires.

But the problem with the new, improved klunkers was the cost. They were expensive, more expensive than the best racing bikes from Italy. Few could afford them.

## The Stumpjumper

Specialized's Stumpjumper changed all that when it debuted in the late summer of 1981. It might not have been as stylish as the custom jobs coming out of artisan shops, but the bike could be had at a decent price, $750, and if it was in the local bike shop, it could be had in hours. Sometimes, though, it took a month, as they were frequently back-ordered.

The Stumpjumper's success demonstrated to the entire American bike industry that there was a market for this thing known as the mountain bike. Soon, every bike company in the United States had to have one in its line. Every shop had to put one in the window. It didn't take long for a few component manufacturers to realize that they needed to make parts for this new market. Profits were suddenly centered on making things for this product.

The Japanese component manufacturers figured out that mountain bikes were a legitimate market before the European manufacturers had a clue. In short order, component giants Shimano and SunTour were no longer selling touring parts for mountain bikes, but actual mountain bike component groups; both companies introduced off-road groups in 1983. Shimano introduced Deore XT, while SunTour debuted their Dirt Component Ensemble. First it was a single line of parts,

Bar-ends, shown in 2001 World Cup action on Canadian Roland Green's bike. His right bar-end is outfitted with a special gear shifter so he can remain on the bar-ends and shift without having to move his hands to the traditional position. Green took second place at the event, held in Vancouver.

then a regular and a pro line, then a regular, pro, and budget. And other companies got into the game as well. SunTour licensed designs from Wilderness Trail Bikes. Guys were making stuff at home and giving it to friends and then selling it to shops. The Italian manufacturers came late to the party, and their parts didn't go far.

This was an exciting time for the mountain bike. Designs evolved fast. Different ideas were tried out all the time. Frame geometries, welding techniques, brake positions, tires, wheels—everything was up for evaluation. The good got copied quickly; a successful frame design would start appearing on other manufacturers' bikes the next year, and component companies would copy and improve their competitors' work. The not-so-good hung around for a few years, waiting to take off or evolve further, and the bad were abandoned.

Klein introduced an aluminum mountain bike frame in 1984. With the exception of Cannondale, which also built exclusively in aluminum, the frame material didn't take off for a long time. Klein also introduced an integrated headset design to work with its oversized steer tube, both of which hit the market in 1989. Almost nobody followed. Both design ideas are popular today. Klein has always had a following, and these people helped keep the company's vision alive.

Index shifting for the rear derailleur became standard on mountain bikes in 1985. Since the custom bikes had quick releases on the seatpost fixing bolt, mass-produced bikes had to have them as well. Handlebar styles went from simple to complex and back again. Sealed bearings became a selling point for the high-end bikes, and they slowly filtered down to the less expensive bikes.

Was the cantilever brake as good as it got? WTB designed a cam brake that SunTour

Giant Team Member Christophe Dupouey shows his typical climbing position using his bar-ends while standing and climbing. Dupouey is a multi-World Cup Champion and World Championship winner.

marketed, while Shimano was selling a U-brake that worked off the same frame fittings. When used as a rear brake, it was mounted under the chain stay. Marketing copy said that this prevented the brakes from filling with mud.

At first, since heavy-duty work boots or hiking shoes were de rigeur for mountain biking, the pedals had to be wide and sharp to grip the shoes well. SunTour's Beartrap pedal was one of the more popular designs, and many companies copied it. The Nike Lava Dome shoe became the shoe of choice—the fast folks put toe clips and straps on the pedals, just like on their road bikes. Pedals got smaller, like on road bikes, and the spikes were smaller.

Meanwhile, the bikes continued to get lighter. Many of the bikes were probably over-built in response to the way that the old Excelsior framesets were breaking. Few—possibly too few—of the early-generation mountain bikes were breaking, so the next logical step was to lighten them.

## Front Suspension

It was inevitable that bicycles would eventually face the suspension issue. Sure, the frames, saddles, handlebars, and stems flex, and wheels absorb shock through tires, tubes, rims, and spokes, but more could be done. As frame builder Chris Chance pointed out, "Look at all other forms of transportation and even the most basic have some kind of suspension

*Designs evolved fast. Different ideas were tried out all the time. Frame geometries, welding techniques, brake positions, tires, wheels—everything was up for evaluation.*

system." Motorcyclists who found mountain bikes fun were getting into design, and they certainly thought that suspension would help riding. In 1987, two ex-motocrossers, Keith Bontrager and Paul Turner, were hired by Kestrel, a carbon-fiber frame builder, to design a full-suspension bike. It was probably never meant for production; instead it was intended to be a show-stopping concept bike.

*Motorcyclists who found mountain bikes fun were getting into design, and they certainly thought that suspension would help riding.*

World Cup Racer Ziranda Madrigal of Mexico races a traditional lightweight cross-country hardtail mountain bike at the 2002 Big Bear NORBA Cross-Country Race at Big Bear, California. This bike has front suspension (no rear suspension), V-Brakes, and a straight handlebar with bar-ends. Madrigal also has a $CO_2$ quick-fill canister taped to his seat post with an extra tube underneath his saddle in case of a tube puncture. Madrigal took second place in this race.

The bike was the Nitro, and it turned heads. Bontrager recalled, "It was the first time I had considered how you could adapt a rear suspension to a bike and make it work." The bike went nowhere, but its designs took off. The front end, the suspension fork, was taken by Turner. He created Rock Shox.

Rock Shox wasn't an immediate success. The fork was heavy, and it looked like it came off a motorcycle. The aesthetic rubbed some cyclists the wrong way. But Turner convinced fast racers to try it, and they won with it. Rock Shox's popularity took off from there. It went from being introduced to market in 1989 to winning the first mountain bike World Championship, on Ned Overend's bike, in 1990.

## Rear Suspension

Rear suspension was a bit harder. "The rear suspension systems interfere with the drivetrain, so the design problem is much harder," Turner said. Unlike the fork, which could easily be added to any bike, rear suspension had to be integral to a frame's design. A custom builder could fabricate a one-off design, but it was incredibly expensive. For rear suspension to take off, it had to be mass-produced. Bike companies weren't afraid of trying out designs; lots of rear-suspension designs were brought to market and sold as the answer to every need, but many had serious deficiencies and took major breakage or complaints to figure out. Bontrager added, "There were a lot of bikes that were functional in one application or another. . . . There were incremental improvements along the way until four or five years ago, and there were a few that worked and a lot that didn't, and things have been sorted."

Cannondale debuted its first rear-suspension bike in 1991, the first production rear-suspension bike. Cannondale's Tom Armstrong recalled, "It had an outrageously high pivot-to-lock out

**Above:** Modern bikes can be equipped to handle anything that today's rides and courses may throw at them.

**Opposite:** Cedric Gracia of the Volvo/Cannondale Factory Team navigates the steep, rocky course at the Vancouver World Cup Downhill Race in 2001. His bike is the Cannondale Gemini. It is not a production bike but rather was made for the Cannondale Race Team. Each year, Gracia and teammate Ann-Caroline Chausson are given one of these bikes, which have a triple clamp DH fork, big tires and rims, disc brakes, and riser handlebars. For this course, Gracia has chosen to use SPD downhill pedals.

suspension when you started pedaling—we thought that was a better idea at the time. . . . There are more abandoned suspension designs than those that endure to this day. I'd be embarrassed if we still showed much of anything we showed in 1991."

The sorting is still in progress, though it's more about refinements than departures. When the mountain bike started, the idea was one bike for all applications. Now, that one bike is seen as a compromise design, as are all suspension designs. Some are for going downhill, some uphill, some both.

## Tech Accessories

A number of parts were created specifically for mountain bikes, and their life spans have varied. At one time, the Hite Rite seat-post spring seemed absolutely necessary. It was a device that allowed the rider to easily drop the seat lower for steep descents, and it would pop back up. These days, while some riders still lower their saddles for a long descent, that isn't the rule.

A longer-standing must-have addition is the bar-end. These horn-shaped things sprout out of the ends of handlebars and give riders a second and possibly third hand position, which eases stress on the hands and allows the rider to use bigger muscles while riding out of the saddle. When they first started appearing in 1989, they took on all forms and shapes. Some companies tried making handlebars with all the curves built in. It turned out that the bars were too tricky. The first, simpler concept was the best.

Kent Eriksen, the frame builder of Moots Cycles, developed the idea in 1982. His idea was wooden knobs on the ends of handlebars. They were called road handles. Onza saw the design, did its own take on it, and the new design took off.

Another feature, Grip Shift, started appearing on bikes in 1987. Index shifting was good, but what about motorcycle twist-style shifting? Initially, Grip Shift was a road bike thing. It started appearing on mountain bikes in 1989, just around the time Shimano introduced its under-the-bar indexed shifters, the Rapidfire. Steve Fairchild, Fuji's product manager, thinks that production capacities limited the initial spread of Grip Shift. "We were one of the first. We did it when some of the other big companies did it, because we couldn't have done it sooner."

Clipless pedals are now standard equipment on mountain bikes. After clipless road pedals came out in 1985, many mountain bikers took their road shoes and pedals and put them on their mountain bikes when they knew that the course called for no dismounts. When they had to walk or run with their bike, touring or cyclocross shoes and clips and straps were put on. Eventually, component giant Shimano developed a recessed cleat that could be worn on shoes that had a walking sole. Shimano designed the whole package: pedal, cleat, and shoe. The SPD (Shimano Pedaling Dynamics) System was introduced in 1990 and found immediate success.

Less successful in the long term were the computer numeric controlled (CNC) anodized bike parts made by boutique shops in the United States. Many of the designs were very good, and the colors looked cool, but the parts were expensive and built in small production runs. As the popularity of CNC-machined parts grew, many small companies with CNC equipment were turning out unique, anodized parts, some good, some bad.

Perhaps Ringlé Components wasn't the first to go the CNC route, but it certainly came up with some of the most popular designs. It debuted a two-bolt stem design for mountain bikes that turned heads and was eventually copied (most bikes have similar stems today). But it wasn't the product that really made

Kona Team rider Geoff Kabush chooses to ride with V-brakes, shown here at the 2001 Napa World Cup in Napa, California.

things happen. Reminiscing about his start in the bike business, Geoff Ringlé looked back. "[The stem] didn't have all the qualities of a hit product, so I decided to analyze all the qualities that made something successful. The skewer was lighter, easy to install, approximately half the weight of existing skewers, basically one part fits all, so that allowed us to do it in color. In about a year, that became incredibly important. Cam-Twist skewers were first."

It was a hit. His company took off from there, developing seat posts, hubs, more stems, water bottle cages, and all in anodized colors. Purple was the hottest.

## When the mountain bike started, the idea was one bike for all applications.

Eventually, the big companies figured out what was right about the parts and either copied or licensed them, and slowly the smaller companies disappeared. Today, you'll still find some shops that are trying to liquidate their purple-anodized components.

Another product that gained acceptance slowly was the threadless headset, or the Aheadset. It was invented by John Rader, and Dia-Compe USA started selling it in 1991. However, the new item didn't work with any of the stems or forks on the market at the time. It was an uphill battle selling it as an aftermarket product. Peter Gilbert, vice president of Cane Creek, Dia-Compe USA's successor, recalled that the product went nowhere at first. "It was a good, solid three years," before it was accepted. Now, most of the bikes in bike shops have it. The trick was to convince bike manufacturers to install it as standard equipment at the factory.

V-brakes, introduced in 1996, were a good solution to the vexing problem of what kind of brake to run on a full-suspension bike. What they ended up creating was a new brake standard for the industry. It wasn't that cantilever brakes worked poorly; they worked well when adjusted right, like most products, but there was something new and right about V-brakes. They took-off and took over within a year or two of introduction.

Just as V-brakes were taking over, disc brakes started gaining acceptance on mountain bikes. Designed similarly to motorcycle disc brakes, the idea had been pioneered by AMP

Research in 1991. Again, one of the major difficulties was the new standard it created. There needed to be a place to attach the brake on the frame as well as hubs that were designed to accept disc brake rotors. At first, they were a rarity, then they were mass-produced beginning in 1997 and slowly found their way onto many bikes—nearly every mountain bike builder has at least one disc brake equipped bike today. They were most popular with downhillers, because the braking was more reliable at high speeds, and the rotor meant they didn't need to limit themselves to rims that had braking surfaces.

### Full Suspension

As mentioned, full suspension took a little while to catch on. Some of the designs were bad, some weren't durable, most were heavy. All were expensive and had no guarantee of being as good as *hardtails* (a reference to motorcycles without rear suspension). There were many riders who doubted that full suspension would ever work well, and there were some purists who didn't like the complexity and cost that came with the designs. But there were enough people willing to buy a bike with unproven designs, and they fueled the market.

Today's full-suspension options are vast. They can be broken down into design differences or intended use. Intended use is easier.

### Downhill Riding

Downhill bikes are designed to go fast on incredibly rough terrain. They are durable and have many inches of travel, both front and rear, and many of the designs are made to maximize control and stability at high speeds. They're also pretty heavy, often close to 40 pounds, like the lightest klunkers, so they're hard to ride uphill. Go to a ski area and take a chairlift to the top: that's your best bet. Brendan Quirk, owner

Thomas Hochstrasser of the Giant World Cup Team races a lightweight full-suspension mountain bike at the Vancouver World Cup in 2002. This bike has front and rear suspension, disc brakes, carbon fiber bar-ends, and a lockout to turn off the rear shock while climbing.

*Previous pages:* Downhill riding provides a thrill a second. Course designers often place several large jumps at the bottom of the course to provide spectators easy access to an exciting viewing area.

of Bikeseller.com, a shop in Little Rock, Arkansas, said of downhill riding, "It's more like downhill skiing in the summertime." These bikes can have upwards of 8 inches of travel on both the front and rear ends of the bike. Disc brakes are pretty much mandatory on downhill bikes, as are single chainrings in the front and chain tensioners.

## Cross-Country Riding

Unlike downhill bikes, these go both up and down. The point of the design is to have enough travel to improve handling and decrease pounding, but not so much as to impede pedaling or that the weight becomes an issue when climbing. The suspension takes the edge off rough riding, but doesn't do much for "big hits" that one can encounter at super-high speed or after catching big air. As a result, there are only a few inches of travel front and rear. These bikes are the lightest of the mountain bike crop, generally weighing in at between 21 and 28 pounds.

It bears mentioning that the classic hardtail is still a pretty popular ride. It's lighter, simpler, and possibly more durable than its full-squishy cousins. Easier to accelerate, fewer things to break, less to think about—all are big pluses of going the classic diamond route. There are plenty of people who prefer going this way, even if there is more pounding transmitted through the frame.

Some folks compromise by getting suspension seat posts. These are posts that allow some travel, either by a sliding stanchion, like on a fork, or a parallelogram linkage. The posts are pretty easy to add or remove at home, so they can be swapped in or out right before a ride.

Canadian Chrissy Redden of the Subaru/Gary Fisher Team uses a lightweight cross-country hardtail mountain bike at the 2002 Big Bear NORBA Cross-Country Race at Big Bear, California. For this race, she chose her hardtail over her fully suspended bike because of the climbing and altitude of this course. This bike also has a traditional straight handlebar and V-Brakes.

Alison Dunlap at the 2002 NORBA Short Track Mountain Bike Race in Big Bear, California, which she won. She also won the 2001 Women's Cross Country World Championship in Vail, Colorado.

**Above:** Robbie Bourdon of the Kona Clump FreeRide Team jumps off a rock on the fabled North Shore of Vancouver. Bourdon's ride has a triple-chain ring that allows him more gears to pedal up hills, front and rear suspension, a riser handlebar, and a triple-clamp fork.

**Opposite:** Joe Schwartz of the Kona Clump FreeRide Team rides down a mountain near Tizirine, Morocco, during filming of *New World Disorder II*.

# What does freeride *mean*, anyway?

## Freeriding

Is it a downhill bike that can climb or a cross-country bike that can ride though big bumps? It occupies the vast middle ground between downhill and cross-country bikes. It's also in the middle in terms of travel and weight. Another problem is the name: What does *freeride* mean, anyway?

Some freeride bikes are kind of like downhill bikes, while others are cross-country bikes that have plenty of travel in the suspension. Six inches of travel is not uncommon in this stable, but unlike their downhill brothers, there are three chainrings so that the bike can go uphill. Unlike cross-country bikes, these bikes usually have heavier, gusseted frames and heavier wheels. Position is different, too. The rider's position is more compact on a freeride bike than on a cross-country bike.

## Mountain Bikes for the Twenty-First Century

What will the next big innovation be? There are designs and components that have been around for a while but are only now catching on. There is always conversation about what are the latest elements on racers' bikes, and other ideas and parts are revealed simply in the hope of generating buzz.

Bikes with adjustable-travel suspension are starting to pop-up. You can now adjust some bikes so that the rear suspension is variable by 2 inches, which can be the difference between just taking the sting out of bumps and sucking up huge holes.

Tubeless tires are an interesting innovation. Only one rim manufacturer and a single tire company worked with it first. But, as the idea has some benefit (lower pressure, no pinch flats), there is interest from riders and tinkerers.

What about all-wheel drive? Weight, friction, and mechanical complications are all issues affecting this idea.

One idea that has been gaining currency for some time is single-speed mountain bikes. The coolest of the lot doesn't possess suspension forks, posts, or rear ends.

There are plenty of other innovations. Just open up a cycling magazine and look around. In the meantime, just ride.

Brett Tippie, the "Godfather of Freeriding," rides the steep slopes of his hometown of Kamloops, British Columbia, Canada.

# goin' ridin'

## where rubber meets dirt

**When mountain bikes** first came about, some folks tried to dub them "all-terrain" bikes, bicycles that could handle anything put beneath them: streets, alleys, sidewalks, gravel, dirt, rocks, mud, sand—you name it, the bikes could take it. The name never stuck, though, perhaps because it wasn't tough enough.

Mountain bikes *can* take on most things. The appeal predates that of the sports utility vehicle, but it is similar. Pretty much everyone first uses their mountain bike on the road. Many never take them into the woods, the bush, the desert, those places where roads don't go. This is a pity, because the riding is most fun where cars can't tread.

John Cowan of the Kona Clump FreeRide Team does a Superman Seat-Grab riding the dirt jumps of San Diego, California. Dirt jumping is a growing segment of the mountain bike community and is where riders take on jumps made of dirt and practice a wide variety of tricks. The mountain bike dirt jumping scene sprouted out from BMX bike culture, and many cyclists from BMX have crossed over to mountain biking and vice versa.

In some ways, mountain biking is everything your parents warned against. Coming home dirty is pretty much a rule for mountain bikers. Before that first ride, test the bike out on the street, driveway, parking lot, or lawn. Make sure it works and be sure you know how to work it. Make sure you can handle basic repairs.

> ### *In some ways, mountain biking is everything your parents warned against.*

Make sure that your skills can handle the ride you're about to take. Don't count on your cell phone saving you when you're in trouble.

## The Road Less Paved

The most basic surface for mountain biking is the unpaved road. In some areas, unpaved roads are a common thing, in other areas they're a rarity. They can be busy thoroughfares or seldom-used jeep trails intended only for emergency purposes. They can be groomed or abandoned. Sometimes, they're smooth hardpack dirt, other times, they're covered with loose gravel. These can be found all over the country, particularly on public land. County, state, and federal government all have reasons for creating roads in

John Cowan rides a berm consisting of the hard-packed red dirt found in San Diego, California.

public land. Sometimes, they're for getting fire-fighting equipment in and out. Sometimes, they're for logging. Sometimes, they're for getting around the reservation, preserve, or park.

The prevailing regional weather conditions must be taken into consideration when choosing roads to ride. Where rain is frequent, the roads can be soft or muddy. Where rain is rare, the roads are often hard and dusty.

Geography often dictates geology as well. Roads next to the Atlantic or Pacific Coasts often have sandy soil. In the Midwest, it's not uncommon to have rock-free dirt, while the Northeast usually has plenty of rocks.

## Trails

Trails are easy to find, even in and around big cities. Ever ride along a road and see a spot right along a curb where the vegetation has disappeared? That spot is often a trailhead. A trailhead is nothing more than a place where a trail begins. You can spy these on maps of public parks or by cruising around parks looking for places where people park their cars. Often, you'll find park rules and trail maps at the park entrance.

But trails aren't always accessed by driving into a park. Some places, it is fine to just dive right into that trail opening by the side of the road. Other places, use caution. Essentially, it is all right to ride on public land, but it isn't wise to tread on private property without permission.

Trails vary widely in terms of terrain and width. Unless you're particularly adventurous and can ride over most anything, it is wise to get some expert advice before trying new trails. Visit a bike shop, find a nearby bike club, look up the park on the Web or in the phone book. Determine if riding is legal, then inquire about the specifics of the riding.

If you're new to the sport, it is wise to start off with easy trails and progress to harder ones as skills develop. It's terrible to confront steep hills and rough trails on your maiden voyage on a mountain bike.

This doubletrack is the part of the racecourse of the Sea Otter Classic Cross-Country Course in Monterey, California. Doubletrack allows racers room to pass and also can provide a sociable setting for recreational riders to ride side by side.

**41**

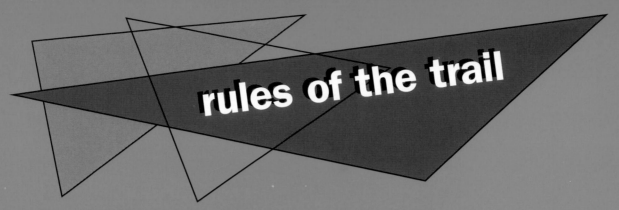

# rules of the trail

"Badges? We don't need no stinkin' badges!" It's an old refrain, and one that seems to go well with the mountain bike. Mountain biking is often about going beyond limits. Mountain bikers aren't loved by everybody, often because of the toll irresponsible riding can take on the land. In order to keep trail access alive, it is best to follow some guidelines to trail riding.

### 1. Ride On Open Trails Only
Respect trail and road closures (ask if uncertain); avoid trespassing on private land; obtain permits or other authorization as may be required. Federal and state wilderness areas are closed to cycling. The way you ride will influence trail management decisions and policies.

### 2. Leave No Trace
Be sensitive to the dirt beneath you. Recognize different types of soils and trail construction; practice low-impact cycling. Wet and muddy trails are more vulnerable to damage. When the trailbed is soft, consider other riding options. This also means staying on existing trails and not creating new ones. Don't cut switchbacks. Be sure to pack out at least as much as you pack in.

### 3. Control Your Bicycle
Inattention for even a second can cause problems. Obey all bicycle speed regulations and recommendations.

### 4. Always Yield Trail
Let your fellow trail users know you're coming. A friendly greeting or bell is considerate and works well; don't startle others. Show your respect when passing by slowing to a walking pace or even stopping. Anticipate other trail users around corners or in blind spots. Yielding means slow down, establish communication, be prepared to stop if necessary and pass safely.

### 5. Never Scare Animals
All animals are startled by an unannounced approach, a sudden movement, or a loud noise. This can be dangerous for you, others, and the animals. Give animals extra room and time to adjust to you. When passing horses use special care and follow directions from the horseback riders (ask if uncertain). Running cattle and disturbing wildlife is a serious offense. Leave gates as you found them, or as marked.

### 6. Plan Ahead
Know your equipment, your ability, and the area in which you are riding—and prepare accordingly. Be self-sufficient at all times, keep your equipment in good repair, and carry necessary supplies for changes in weather or other conditions. A well-executed trip is a satisfaction to you and not a burden to others. Always wear a helmet and appropriate safety gear.

These Rules of the Trail are from the International Mountain Biking Association's Web site, www.imba.com.

IMBA was created to deal with the threat of trail closure. Started in California in 1988, it is now truly an international group. IMBA has many guidelines for sensible trail riding, including the IMBA code, which is a mantra to many cyclists.

## Doubletrack

Essentially a narrow road wide enough for one car, doubletrack is known for the two tracks that the left and right wheels of a car or truck impressed upon the ground. These are sometimes known as jeep cuts or fire roads. These are usually wide enough that two cyclists can ride next to each other. Of course, the rocks, ruts, puddles, and branches up ahead might prevent a simple side-by-side ride.

## Singletrack

Singletrack is mountain biker heaven on Earth. In the words of Pete Webber, IMBA's communications director, "The Holy Grail is singletrack. Singletrack is really what most mountain bikers are looking for. It's the ultimate mountain biking route. We say 'like singletrack to cyclists, like powder to skiers,' like the perfect wave to surfers. It's what most mountain bikers are seeking."

A piece of classic singletrack in the remote regions of southwest British Columbia, Canada. This singletrack has all the ingredients of a classic ride—high elevation, great views, and a very smooth surface.

John Cowan rides singletrack right next to the ocean in Carlsbad, California. This hard, compressed sand makes for good trail-riding conditions and drains well following a rain.

*Hop the rock, ride over the root, avoid the branch, jump the puddle, thread the needle, break a sweat. . . . But take it easy. Singletrack can be intense, and that's a kind of fun that many dig.*

Singletrack is a trail as wide as a set of handlebars. It can be straight and flat or curvy and mountainous, or straight and mountainous or curvy and flat. It varies dramatically. The singletrack rides that are deemed the most fun challenge the rider's bike handling skills and make it feel as though you're cutting a swath into a pristine wilderness. Hop the rock, ride over the root, avoid the branch, jump the puddle, thread the needle, break a sweat. . . . But take it easy. Singletrack can be intense, and that's a kind of fun that many dig.

## What Lies Beneath

Whereas pavement is consistent, dirt comes in many forms. Just like there is a difference between the dirt on the infield at Yankee Stadium and the diamond behind the local high school, there are great differences in topsoil.

## Dirt

This is a huge category. Sometimes the dirt is so dense, dry, and hard, it might as well be pavement. Other times, it's soft and loose. Riding is different in each case, and getting a feel is part of the sport.

Trail advocates generally like riders to minimize skidding. Skidding can be fun, but it can rip-up trails and cause erosion, which permanently damages terrain.

## Mud

There is something irresistible about mud. Once stained by a little, soaked by a lot doesn't seem like a bad deal. Whether it's thick or watery, mud is out there, waiting to splatter. Some people like to ride the edges, while others plow right through. It takes power to push through.

Mike MacDonnell rides rough, jagged rocks along the Lake Minnewanka Trail in Banff National Park, Alberta, Canada.

Richard Cox rides through a rocky section of trail in Canmore, Alberta, Canada.

## Rocks

There are rocks and then there are *rocks:* There are pebbles, small- to mid-sized boulders, giant boulders, and sheets of rock, to name a few. Some are mere annoyances, while others can stop a bike in its tracks. The small stuff is easy not to sweat, except when the trails are steep and the rocks loose. A rock in the wrong place can cause wheels to slip. The big stuff can be easy to ride over, provided the rocks are dry. Beware! Slippery when wet.

## Sand

According to John Brigan, president of the Ocala Mountain Bike Association (OMBA), "Native Floridians give is 'the sand is our mountains,' i.e., it's as difficult as pedaling up hill." It's easy to slide on the microrocks, and too much of it can be nearly impossible to ride.

## Frozen Expanse

Snow and ice seem like obstacles a mountain bike should easily handle. Mountain bikes can be great fun on the frozen whites, but this isn't always the case. Snow that is too deep and fluffy is impossible to get a grip on with regular mountain bike knobbies. Ice is always slippery.

Snowbound mountain bikers have developed solutions, and some are similar to the

Steve Walker and his dog Jagger enjoy a winter outing on the frozen Bow River in Calgary, Alberta, Canada. Special metal-studded bike tires provide excellent traction and allow riders to explore frozen lakes and rivers.

Kyle Biggy shows good snow-riding form, keeping his weight on the rear wheel to avoid an endo while riding down a patch of deep snow. This is summer at high elevation in Kananaskis Country, Alberta, Canada.

response to sand. Ultrawide tires and wheels help the bikes float on the snow. Studded tires, which can either be bought or made, run great on ice. Like the brain trust behind the beginning of the mountain bike, where there's a will, there's a way. Creative solutions manifest themselves on the trail.

## Places to Ride

Most mountain bikers look at the world as open for riding, unless explicitly stated otherwise. It's not a bad philosophy, and one that the American legal system generally supports. But the various land agencies don't always see it that way. Jenn Dice, IMBA's advocacy director, sees it this way. "[T]here is really no general rule about trails being open unless designated closed or closed unless designated open. Each major land management agency has a different philosophy. For example, the U.S. Forest Service and Bureau of Land Management are open unless closed. National Park Service and U.S. Fish and Wildlife lands are closed unless open. I am not sure what the Army Corps of Engineers attitude is, but I would bet it is open unless closed, as they are very recreation minded. Their chief of recreation spoke at our conference asking for mountain bikers to volunteer and build trails on their land.

"If in doubt, we encourage cyclists to talk to land managers first, especially if an area is in question, has high traffic volume, or user conflict of any kind. Some trails are so remote that no one cares and there aren't resources to sign them according to appropriate user groups."

John Cowan of the Kona Clump FreeRide Team does a No Hander while dirt jumping in Loule, Portugal.

## Ski Areas

Ski areas have become a haven for summertime mountain biking. Over 150 downhill ski centers offer mountain biking in the green months. Since the land is either privately held or publicly owned with an understanding that the ground has been deforested and taken away from nature, there are few restrictions on mountain biking. The marriage is made good by resorts looking to score some extra cash during their slow season. No matter the reason why, ski areas do offer many riding options. Most offer several choices: a pass for riding the trails, or for a single chair-lift ride to the top, or just for taking the lifts. Many offer equipment rentals and lessons. While the ski area may look extreme, the people running the place have usually found a way to have some easy trails for novices.

Are, Sweden, is a popular ski resort in Scandinavia that runs its chair lifts and gondola for skiers in the winter and for mountain bike riders in the summer. This photo was taken during the World Mountain Bike Championships in 1999. The chairs are outfitted with special brackets to allow bikes to hang beside the rider on the way up.

## Street Riding

Pretty much every bike gets ridden on streets. Pavement is the coin of our auto-dominated realm. It is common for beginners to believe that mountain bikes are the best ride for city streets. They might be, but not as set-up for mountain biking. Suspension needs to be stiffened or locked out, as the bumps are small. Knobby tires should be traded for slicks; fat tires for skinnier ones.

But, if transportation isn't your angle—tricks are the order—then go back and whip out the freeride bike (though any mountain bike should suffice). Urban riding is BMX freestyle for grown-ups. The bigger wheels and full suspension make more things possible. The best places to go are the concrete and steel canyons of downtown, especially after hours and on weekends. Stairs, drop-offs, tabletops, ledges, and other feats of insanity are best accomplished on

Vancouver, British Columbia, Canada is world famous for its mountain bike trails, but it also offers good routes for bike commuters. There are also bike/pedestrian lanes across its major bridges. Many bike couriers choose mountain bikes for their versatility, rugged tires, and frames that can withstand years of abuse.

## Urban riding is BMX freestyle for grown-ups.

freeride bikes. North Shore, urban trick riding done on the North Shore of Vancouver, British Columbia, is becoming a style unto its own.

### Cross-Country

This is where mountain biking really began. A go-anywhere, do-anything trip where human power could take a bike up a mountain as well as down. This is what mountain biking had to offer for most of its first decade. Sometimes, it seems quaint, but the prospect of riding hours in the woods is probably best accomplished on a cross-country bike. While riding over everything is preferable, some walking is probably inevitable. Trails change, and fallen trees, a recent landslide, or rain can dramatically change a trail from one ride to the next.

### Freeride

Freeride is a somewhat nebulous term. It is pretty much everything that cross-country riding and downhilling aren't. The term *freeride* was really a creation of mountain bike manufacturers to describe a new class of bikes that was seeing increased demand. A freeride bike has more gears to pedal up steep hills, yet a big frame to handle the downhills. Freeride bikes are generally lighter than downhill race bikes so as to be easier to handle on technical trails and to facilitate stunt riding.

For some, freeriding is about the tricks. For others, it's doing some climbing to get to the fun, nutty descent. For certain, freeride bikes are more versatile and more capable of handling all kinds of terrain and riding.

Scott Grieve rides the scenic Windy Pass Trail in the Chilcotin Mountains of British Columbia, Canada.

Robbie Bourdon of the Kona Clump FreeRide Team rides off a cliff in Morocco during the filming of *New World Disorder II*, an extreme mountain bike movie.

***Opposite and above:*** John Cowan negotiates a tricky route in Laguna Beach, California.

Joe Schwartz rides down a steep pitch in Oukaimeden, Morocco, during filming of *New World Disorder II*.

## Downhill

This discipline is all about working with gravity. It is often practiced at alpine ski areas, where riders can take the chairlift up to go zipping down. Ski areas aren't the only places that can accommodate the thrill downhill junkies seek.

Many riders simply find an access road to the top of a steep decline in the area of their choice. Still others simply push their bikes up the biggest hill or mountain they can find and ride them back down.

A rider takes on the infamous Kamikaze downhill course at Mammoth Mountain, California. One of the first downhill race courses to gain notoriety, this racecourse was originally just an access road that wound itself to the top of Mammoth Mountain Ski Resort. Top speeds on this course usually hover just over 60 miles per hour on the long straightaway, where this photo was taken. Race organizers also ran an uphill mass start cross-country race, which retraced the downhill course uphill.

## Touring

Mountain bike touring is an alternative to road touring. Just like on the road, the cyclist can either hook up panniers or a trailer and do it self-supported or link-up with a tour company and have sag wagon support, or even partial sag support. The difference is that one can get further away from civilization touring on a mountain bike. It can be as gentle or as extreme as the rider wants. The extreme side can be done almost anywhere, but the gentle stuff is largely limited in the United States to the western states, where there are vast tracts of government-owned land and countless miles of rarely used unpaved roads.

One of the best known off-road touring routes in the United States is the Great Divide Route, mapped by the Adventure Cycling Association. This 2,500-mile off-road route rides along the continental divide from Canada to Mexico. It can be done solo or with a group, supported or self-sufficient.

## Tandem

Mountain bike tandems have been produced for a long time but in small batches by only a few producers. It is unusual to see them, and doubly so on the trail. Most mountain bike tandems are valued for their heavy-duty frames and wheels and their upright position, and they are ridden on the road.

Still, people do take them into the wilderness, and the bikes are built with parts that might look at home on motorcycles. For some, the reason to ride is as easy as, "Why not?" They like the variety. But Jack Goertz, editor of *Doubletalk* magazine, noted, "It gives you a good chance for two of you to get into nature without losing your partner. You've got a partner to get through the bad stuff, and can enjoy the good. You can't lose them on the downhill." Still, he knows it isn't easy. Lots of coordination and conversation has to go on to move a bike that big through singletrack and over rough stuff. Tandems are too long to handle super-tight switchbacks, but Goertz thinks that they can get through most anything else.

There are even a few off-road tandem rallies in the United States, where dedicated mountain-biking tandemers get together for some group tandeming. One of the most popular is the FART, the Fall Allegany Rally for Tandems.

## Night Riding

Night riding is a category unto itself. Any bike can be taken night riding. The bike isn't the issue. Rather, light, or the lack thereof, is. It is possible to go mountain biking off-road at night without lights, but one pretty much has to have the vision of a cat to pull it off and see in three dimensions. In some other conditions, it would be possible to ride off-road in the dark, but there aren't too many.

The solution is a lighting system. Throwing "system" in there is an indication that it takes more than a flashlight taped to the handlebars to ride safely at night. It generally takes a high-tech, high-powered flashlight, usually with a halogen bulb and a mega-battery, to ride at night. Some people use a handlebar-mounted light with a huge battery that goes in a water bottle cage, while others carry the battery in a big pocket and mount the light to the helmet. Some choose to do both. "Juice," or burn time, that is, battery life (thank goodness these batteries are rechargeable), becomes the big limiter at night. It is best to know the route, or have someone who does, and make sure that the time it takes to complete the ride is a good bit less than the burn time on the battery. Even though there are low-power settings to utilize and spare batteries to carry, flats, wrong turns, and gremlins can spell trouble.

Night riding is a big thrill, though not for everyone. The woods at night are dark and spooky, not a place where most people go for fun. The excitement is enhanced by the

*Night riding is a big thrill, though not for everyone. The woods at night are dark and spooky, not a place where most people go for fun.*

Richard Cox tours the backcountry near Whistler, British Columbia, Canada, while carrying his lightweight sleeping bag and food in a backpack. Extra tools, tubes, and a first-aid kit are essential to ensure a successful trip.

fact that it is almost impossible to see beyond the beam's glare. Speeds are slower, handling is a bit trickier, and the concentration needed to ride well is incredible.

When taking a breather, it is a good idea to switch off the lights. Suddenly, the world is dark. Noises not noticed while riding suddenly pop up everywhere. Where's the trail? Both what has been and what will be is nowhere to be found. Moonlight filters in. The wilderness is alive.

For all the reasons above, most go night riding in a group. It's more than a workout. It's a social occasion. Instead of going for a beer, folks go for a ride. The beer can always be had later.

Another dimension to the excitement is the legality of night riding. Some places it is fine, others, verboten. The main reason is for safety. Don't expect help getting out—one more reason night riding is only for the most experienced and self-sufficient of riders.

Cyclists competing in the 24 Hours of Adrenalin bike event tag-off to their teammates in the middle of the night. Riders attach lights to their helmets or bikes or sometimes both. Night riding brings added elements of excitement and risk to mountain biking.

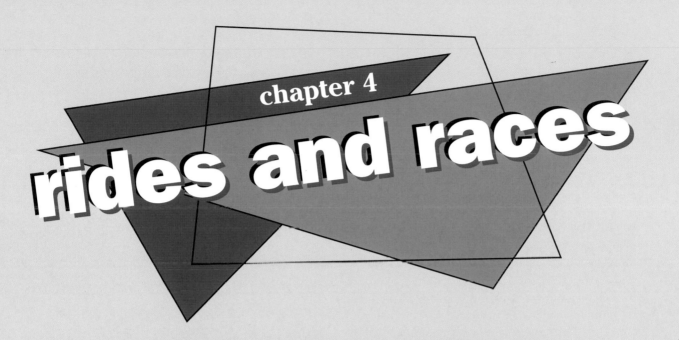

# chapter 4
# rides and races

## breathe hard and have fun

**Whether you choose** to ride or race, or both, there are countless ways for you to pedal and barrel until your legs and mind are content. Check out these suggestions, talk to your friends and fellow riders, and roll whenever and wherever you please!

**Riding**

Riding is easy: sling a leg over and go. But riding can get lonely, sometimes it is hard to find trails alone, and you may improve faster if there are others to teach you a thing or two, even if it is by osmosis. Lots of people ride, and

The Mountain Bike Festival in Riva del Garda, Italy, is the biggest mountain bike festival in Europe. It features a huge exposition area, parties, races, and the very popular lake-jumping event, held at night.

lots of people would like a fellow rider to explore with. So everyone get together and go kick some trail!

## Shop Rides

Shops put on shop rides because their employees are usually cyclists who either ride before or after work, and if they're going out, they might as well bring some friends. Some shops see this as savvy marketing, a way of increasing customers' bonds to the store, but it's a ride all the same. The rides can be instructive, almost rolling classes. Regardless, the shop is usually a good meeting place. There's almost always a bathroom, a place to change, and last-minute doohickeys and snacks. The employees are usually skilled cyclists who have the inside line on the latest equipment (they are happy to dish on both the good and the bad) and the good trails.

## Club Rides

Clubs are usually bigger and more ambitious than bike shops. Members might live in different places, and they'll look for longer rides, particularly for weekends. The good thing about clubs is that they increase your exposure to the sport through meetings, newsletters, Web sites, and electronic mailing lists. And, of course, the members will take you on rides you wouldn't have found any other way.

You can find clubs through bike shops or on the Web, or through national organizations such as the League of American Bicyclists (LAB), a bike lobby; USA Cycling/National Off-Road Bicycling Association (NORBA), the national governing body of bike racing in the United States; and IMBA. There are also regional and state-based organizations: Michigan has the Michigan Mountain Bike Association (MMBA), Oregon has the Oregon Bicycle Racing Association (OBRA), and New England has the Eastern Fat Tire Association (EFTA).

## Epics

Epics are the rides we hate to love and love to hate. You may have experienced one already: a ride too far; a day you got horribly lost, and the weather changed for the worse; or a day when everything that could go wrong did go wrong. Other times, epics are planned in advance. The planned epic is one that is wildly ambitious and incredibly hard, a ride that deserves celebration afterward. Eat well, drink up. You'll be both hungry and thirsty at the end.

> *The planned epic is one that is wildly ambitious and incredibly hard, a ride that deserves celebration afterward.*

IMBA has taken this concept and turned it into organized events, with both trailwork before and a great ride after.

EFTA has similar rides, but with a less-threatening name: Fun Rides. The courses are marked, so there's no need to keep up with a group, and a map is handed out at the start, so even if things are confusing, there's a way to get back.

## Festivals

Pedro's, the lube company, has demonstrated how incredible a large-scale organized event can be. In 1995, Pedro's came up with the idea of a festival as a way to have a non-race party at the end of the season. Pedro's Mountain Bike Festivals are three days of riding, camping, and hanging out. According to Karl Wiedemann, Pedro's communications director, "It's just a good, relaxing atmosphere to hang out with friends. Everyone is sharing a common bond, which is a mountain bike, and they're doing common rides that their ability will hold." A big party with riding as the theme is a great way to spend a long weekend. Pedro's currently has two festivals going, one on the East Coast and one in the Midwest, but there are others out there. The Sea Otter Classic in California is another weekend cycling extravaganza. It has top-flight road and mountain bike racing, as well as rides, classes, contests, and an equipment expo.

> *A big party with riding as the theme is a great way to spend a long weekend.*

## Weekends

There are also organized mountain bike weekends. Some travel companies put these on, but with a little planning and foresight, a group of friends can put one together, too. Usually, all that's needed is access to park trails and either tents or some lodging. Local bike shops usually have plenty of trail maps to reference, and the Web offers an almost endless amount of resources for great rides in just about every area.

## Vacations

When a weekend just isn't long enough to get all the mountain bike cravings out, there are always mountain bike vacations. Here, too, you have options that vary between totally unsupported to lavishly supported. A vacation can be as simple as hanging out at a state park or ski area or as ambitious as riding unsupported

The Sea Otter Classic, held each year in the spring in Monterey, California, is North America's biggest bike festival. Thousands of professional and recreational cyclists compete in road and mountain bike events. The festival is staged at the Laguna Seca Raceway, famous for car and motorcycle racing. This picture shows the start of the men's dirt criterium event, where the riders compete on a short circuit for one hour. The mountain bike stage race features a time trial, the dirt criterium, and the cross-country race.

through a wilderness. On many trips, a gear truck carries the heavy stuff from campsite to campsite while the riders cycle in between. While it may sound cushy, the riding isn't easy, though many tour companies are known for cooking great food at the end of the day.

## Racing

Non-racers talk about bike racing with a certain qualification: racers are "serious." It is hard to say if they are more serious than non-racers, but it can be said that they like their rides timed and in a manner that compares them with other racers. It takes training to do well, but it will always be recreational at heart—too few people make a living at it for racing to be anything else. Friends race friends up and down mountains all the time. They also compare how well they rode a part of tricky trail. Racing is simply more formal. The formality helps further the skills that make mountain bike riding fun. Maybe the pro racers train only because they have to. For all others, the training is most of what they do; the racing is merely the excuse.

Mountain bike racing takes place all over the country, even in places without mountains. Racing can be a year-round sport.

In the United States, the national governing body is the National Off-Road Bicycling Association (NORBA). It's part of USA Cycling, which also controls most road racing and a good chunk of the BMX racing in the United States. The folks at NORBA put together the national team and teams for international events, like the Olympics. To race in a NORBA race, one must have a NORBA license, which can be purchased for the day or year.

Even though NORBA is nationwide, there are many regional and state organizations that also sanction racing. Usually, the major difference between a state organization and NORBA is that the smaller groups provide less-expensive insurance and fewer regulations, which can make event promotion easier. For the cyclist, the major difference turns up when looking at races. Each group has its own calendar.

## Cross-Country

Cross-country is the most basic form of racing. It is a mass-start event, with lots of riders going over the same course at the same time. The name suggests that the racing is point-to-point, but such races are very hard to manage and even harder to close trails for. Most cross-country racing takes place on a circuit that is covered between one and several times over the course of the race. It is not uncommon for the newest cross-country racers to only complete one lap for fear that they can't handle the distance or the intensity of longer racing. Circuits can be as short as 2 or 3 miles and as long as, well, long. Maybe a 200-mile loop is the long end.

*It is not uncommon for the newest cross-country racers to only complete one lap for fear that they can't handle the distance or the intensity of longer racing.*

*Opposite:* Racers preride the course at the Napa World Cup in Napa, California. Racers are usually allowed to train on the racecourse only at specific times prior to race days so no cyclist will have an advantage over the other competitors.

66

*Above:* The Senior Elite Men's Cross-Country Race course at the Sea Otter Classic in Monterey, California.

*Left:* Mass start at the Men's World Mountain Bike Race held in Mont-Sainte-Anne, Quebec, Canada 1997. The riders are placed on the start line grid according to their World Cup ranking as of the previous race. The highest-ranked riders start farther ahead than lower-ranked riders. This provides a real advantage to the best riders, as they are the first to hit the singletrack sections of the race course, whereas the riders placed farther back have to fight to get ahead. Cross-country races usually start on an open section that funnels down to the singletrack after an initial start lap.

Ryder Hesjedal, of Canada, wins the 2000 Big Bear NORBA Short Track Race in Big Bear, California. The short-track event is unique to the NORBA circuit and was designed to generate spectator interest in the sport of cross-country mountain bike racing. NORBA races are usually held at downhill ski areas to provide ski lift access to the downhill racers. The short-track events are usually held at the base area of the mountain, and in the case of the Big Bear race, the circuit goes through the ski village itself, providing easy access to spectators. Short-track races take place the day after the cross-country race, and there is a separate overall classification and points leader for the short-track and cross-country races.

## Short-Track

Short-track racing is mountain biking's equivalent to road biking's criterium racing. It's also known as dirt crits. The circuits are very short, about one to three minutes in length, and fast. It is faster and more tactically oriented than a traditional cross-country race. Short-track races are different than cross-country races, but generally they're put on as spectator-friendly events at the national level.

The Men's Pro Dirt Criterium Event held at the Sea Otter Classic in 1999. The Sea Otter Classic is a stage race held at the Laguna Seca Raceway near Monterey, California. This event features three separate races on three consecutive days. The first is the time trial, where riders start separately at one-minute intervals and go for the fastest time. Day two is the Dirt Criterium, shown here, where racers go around a short race loop for one hour only. On the third day is the cross-country race, where the racers do two laps of a large cross-country course. Each cyclist is given a ranking according to his time after every stage, and the overall winner is decided on a combined-time scoring system.

## Downhill

Downhill is a timed race that's all about descending. Often, these are run at ski areas, where the racers get a lift to the top. Most of the time, they are run like ski races or time trials, with one racer out of the gate at a time and racers competing to have the fastest time. Occasionally, there will be multiple racers competing against each other on the same course at the same time.

## Hillclimb

Uphill events used to be a regular part of big mountain bike race weekends. They now pop- up only occasionally. While they can be run as time trials, many of them were run as mass-start events. Unlike downhill, they don't generate the excitement that speed delivers. It takes lungs, legs, and great balance to do well at these.

## Observed-Trials

Observed-trials racing is something we all can appreciate. In a trial, one is supposed to go from point A to point B, usually a very short distance such as a few feet, and go over, under, around, or through the obstacles without touching a foot, hand, elbow, or head to anything other than the bike. Traditionally, these events consist of five to ten sections. A "dab" is touching something other than the bike. And each time a foot, hand, elbow, etc., dabs, it costs points. Each section is worth five points if cleared perfectly within the time limit, which is usually three minutes or less. Each dab costs a point, and standing still for too long

Marklof Berchtold of the Global Team navigates the tricky, steep NORBA course at Big Bear, California in 2002. Downhill courses usually have a wide array of difficult obstacles, steep sections, and jumps that challenge the riders. Riders race one at a time at one-minute intervals and are given training periods at specific times leading up to race day. On race day, there is a seeding run in the morning, where all the racers must qualify for the main event in the afternoon. The fastest rider in the qualifying round starts last in the actual race.

Nicolas Vouilloz wins the 2002 Avalanche Cup held in Lyon, France. France has usually lead the way in the sport of downhill racing, and its national series is called the Avalanche Cup. At the Lyon race, thousands of people fill the area to cheer their favorite racers. Vouilloz is a national hero and has dominated the sport of downhill mountain bike racing since he was a junior.

costs a point as well. The person with the highest total wins. There are events for stock bikes, the regular mountain bike one can find at a bike shop, as well as events for trials bikes, which are bikes built specifically for this type of event.

### Dual Slalom

Dual slalom is very similar to the ski event of the same name. Two riders start simultaneously at the top of parallel downhill courses and have to weave around identical sets of gates. The first person across the line at the bottom is the winner. The riders are seeded and move through a bracket in the way that single-elimination tournaments in soccer and tennis take place. This was a popular World Championship event for a number of years, but the International Cycling Union (UCI) ended it after 2001. Even without World Championship status, it is still a popular event in some places.

### Mountain Cross, a.k.a. 4-Cross or 4X

The UCI replaced dual slalom with mountain cross at the start of 2002. It is similar to downhill in that the event is boosted by gravity. It is similar to dual slalom in that it is comprised of

Mike King and Cedric Gracia sprint to the finish at the 2002 Sea Otter Classic Dual Slalom event in Monterey, California. Dual slalom is a timed event, where two cyclists race side by side, on separate courses, against the clock. Racers usually take part in a seeding run in the morning, when they are timed against the clock to determine who is the fastest for the main event. In the afternoon, they race head-to-head, taking a turn on each course to determine the winner of that heat. It is a basic knockout formula, where the winner proceeds onward and the losers do not continue. Gracia won this race and the overall title at the 2002 Sea Otter Dual Slalom Event.

elimination heats that move competitors forward in the event. Four racers start down the course at the same time. The first two to the finish line move on to the next round. Sometimes, the third-place rider in the heat is allowed to move on to a round for a final chance at advancing. In all cases, the fourth rider is out of the competition.

## Mountain Bike Duathlons/Triathlons

These races are a lot like the duathlons and triathlons known around the world, only they replace asphalt with dirt, grass, and woods. They also come in a number of flavors. Some are loosely organized events, while others are big and sponsored. There are plenty of unusual smaller events that combine mountain biking with another sport. According to USA Triathlon, the governing body for triathlons in the United States, they sanction bike-canoe events as well as bike-orienteering events and others.

Among the big events is the Xterra Series, which presented itself as a hybrid of mountain bike cool and triathlon intensity. The name might be familiar because the Nissan Motor Company licensed the name for a car it produces. Mountain bike legend Ned Overend retired from mountain bike racing and started

*Above and right:* In an effort to generate fan interest and television coverage of mountain bike racing, race organizers started mountain bike cross as a test event in 2001. A full NORBA and World Cup schedule was adopted in 2002. Four racers start at the same time and race the same course, with the top two racers advancing in each heat. A more exciting and dangerous version of the dual events of the past, mountain bike cross has been a controversial addition to the downhill discipline. It has created interest in the sport, but the injury count has been mounting throughout its first year.

doing these in his "retirement." There are now national championships in these events. They're sanctioned by USA Triathlon. Xterra is very mountain biker friendly, according to the promoters, who point out that 65 percent of the event is on the bike.

## 24-Hour

Twenty-four hour racing is a bike racing idea that predates mountain biking. Extreme tests of this sort have been going on as long as there has been racing. In the 1890s, a racing discipline called the Six-Day was popular. It was a six-day race on a velodrome, a bicycle track. Competitors would race 24 hours a day for six days straight. These events were popular into the 1930s. Long single-event races starting in one city and finishing in another city were also popular.

For mountain biking, 24-hour racing more or less started in 1992, when Laird Knight decided to run an event called the 24 Hours of Canaan. Held in West Virginia, the event drew 36 four- or five-person teams. The event was fun and was a success. It had night riding, and it was a weekend of racing and hanging with friends. Last year, the 24 Hours of Snowshoe, Canaan's successor, had 550 teams.

Two years later, Tri-Life Sports debuted the 24 Hours of Adrenalin. This series has been extremely popular. Tri-Life Sports promoted 12 events in 2002.

In 2001, there were nearly 50 24-hour races, not only in the United States, but also in Canada and all around the globe. While most of the races emphasize team racing, there are solo races.

Teams make racing easier and more fun for friends to do together. The circuits are usually long enough that it can take more than an hour per lap. Each teammate does a lap on, three- to five-laps rest, another lap on. In the interim, there is eating, sleeping, and hanging out.

*In 2001, there were nearly 50 24-hour races, not only in the United States but also in Canada and all around the globe.*

## Extreme

For some, racing isn't fun unless the race is painfully long and absurdly difficult. For these people, there are extreme races. There aren't too many of these around, but those in the know have heard of them and either fear them or dismiss these events as havens for nutcases. Extreme races are the kind of thing where competitors must check their sanity at the door, unless it seems like fun. Then, you're the nutcase.

One long-running example is the Iditasport in Alaska. Started as the Iditabike in 1987, it was a 200-mile winter bike race on the Iditarod Trail outside of Anchorage. Currently, there is a shorter, 130-mile Iditasport and a much longer Iditasport Extreme event that can take over five days to complete.

There are other extreme races. Every region seems to have a few 100-mile races every year. There are multi-day, multi-discipline events—like the Raid Gauloises—for the truly committed and heavily sponsored.

Randy Spangler competes in the Whistler Joyride Dirt Jump Competition in Whistler, British Columbia, Canada. Dirt jumping competitions are relatively new to the sport of mountain biking. Competitors are given several jumps to gain points from a panel of judges and are awarded points for various tricks and their degree of difficulty.

*Opposite:* The sport of twenty-four hour racing has taken off in the sport of mountain bike racing. Teams of riders or solo competitors race for twenty-four consecutive hours on the same course, starting at noon on Saturday and finishing at noon on Sunday. Twenty-four hour racing has injected enthusiasm into the recreational racing scene and does not show signs of slowing down. Competitors camp on the race site, and the scene has a lighthearted festival atmosphere. Serious solo competitors usually ride nonstop and top mountain bike professionals are now becoming involved, giving this discipline credibility and respect in the mountain bike community. The races begin with a "LeMans Start," where the cyclists run several hundred yards to their bikes before they start cycling.

chapter 5

# legends

# mountain biking's public faces

**The mountain bike** world is filled with characters. They shaped the sport by accident, by luck, and by force of personality. Chapters 1 and 2 give a sense of the rider/designer/thinker/tinkerers who started riding and brought the mountain bike to the world. Every region had a colorful guy or gal who was the person to go to when seeking mountain bike wisdom. Sometimes, that person was a shop employee, sometimes a promoter, and very often a racer.

Racers are frequently the public face of a sport. On the road, Lance Armstrong and Greg LeMond sold road cycling to the United States. In this chapter, we'll take a less than definitive look at a few of the faces that sold off-road cycling.

Mountain bike legend Missy Giove races the downhill at the 1998 World Cup in Big Bear, California.

## Victor Vicente of America (VVA)

In many ways, it seems like the early promoters of the sport were a little more colorful than their contemporary brethren. Maybe it is because the new and unusual attracts unusual characters or maybe because the unusual is simply accentuated by doing something far out. For VVA, it could be both.

*Mike Hiltner puts on big miles for a 61-year-old, sometimes upwards of 300 a week.*

Long ago, VVA was known as Mike Hiltner, a top road racer who raced in the 1960 and 1964 Olympics and tried his hand at pro racing in Europe. Eventually, he returned to the United States, re-christened himself VVA, and embarked on a life as a cyclist, a bike designer, an artist working in many media, a bike race promoter, and mountain bike diarist.

He traces his beginning in mountain biking to 1978, when he found a dirt road that connected Los Angeles' Mulholland Drive, a road that runs along a ridge above Los Angeles. Without knowing of the bikes being built and modified far north in Marin County, he came up with his own design, the Topanga!, something he called "an adult-sized multi-geared mudster." He also tried selling them as a commercial venture.

In 1980, he became a mountain bike race promoter, putting on the Reseda to the Sea race and Puerco! The former was a point-to-point race in a national park, and the latter was a three-mile hill climb and downhill. Reseda was run as a race, then as an unofficial race, until 1996. There was also a Mt. Wilson Hillclimb and Downhill and a number of others, and all but

one were put on in the mountains of Santa Monica. In the early days, Mike raced his own events, occasionally as the only registered competitor.

He also spread the gospel of mountain biking through his newsletter, the *Topanga Riders' Bulletin*. It was published from 1980 through 1996, and VVA is proud of doing all the production without the aid of a computer.

VVA's exploits have landed him in both the United States Bicycling Hall of Fame and the Mountain Bike Hall of Fame. Currently, he lives in Northern California, where he works on his art—which is pretty much all bike-related—and rides. VVA puts on big miles for a 61-year-old, sometimes upwards of 300 a week.

## Jacquie Phelan

Jacquie Phelan is one of the few riders to bridge the early denim-clad days to the established sport. She was there in the early days in Marin County, just as mountain bikes were becoming mountain bikes, living in San Francisco and getting around without a car. She rode with the guys and got good. As mountain bike racing wasn't officially around in 1981, she started road racing and showed talent, scoring a fourth at the National Road Championships. In 1983, with sanctioned racing having just gotten off the ground, Phelan won the first-ever women's NORBA Nationals. She dominated the fledgling sport for the next two years, and stayed at the

*When there weren't enough women to compete against, Phelan took on the men, often doing quite well and occasionally winning.*

One of mountain biking's founders and member of the Mountain Bike Hall of Fame, Jacquie Phelan plays the banjo during the 2000 Napa World Cup in Napa, California.

top for the rest of the decade. When there weren't enough women to compete against, Phelan took on the men, often doing quite well and occasionally winning.

As mountain bike racing shifted into high gear, Phelan was riding past her competitive peak and ultimately settled into racing veterans classes, going to the World Championships in her age bracket, and promoting the sport.

It turned out that her personality was as strong as her riding skills. She became known for the pink polka-dot tights worn under her shorts, colored streamers in her braids, outrageous stunts (finishing a race topless), and for her alter ego, Alice B. Toeclips.

She founded the Women's Mountain Bike and Tea Society (WOMBATS) in 1984, a group that still exists and still conducts camps. A WOMBAT, Susan De Mattei, medaled at the first women's mountain bike race in the Olympics. Jacquie is also known as a mountain bike journalist, penning articles in a number of languages, and as a commentator and public speaker.

## Ned Overend

Overend was, and is, so good that most overlooked the fact that his name was perfectly sport specific. Overend was a top road racer in the 1980s, when he moved to Durango, Colorado. In 1983, Overend was also working at Durango's Mountain Bike Specialists bike shop, and he decided to try out mountain biking. He liked it enough to leave the road behind. Unlike many of the early riders, who were downhillers first and foremost, Overend was all about lungs and climbing. Just as mountain biking was being established as a sport, he was a sponsored pro, something of a rarity. He quickly moved to the top of the sport, where he stayed for several years. He won six national championships between 1986 and 1992, and in 1990, he won the inaugural Mountain Bike World Championships in his hometown of Durango, Colorado. His place in history was set.

Never a guy to look back, Overend was a threat for years to come. He was one of the last American men to win a World Cup race in Europe, which he did twice in 1994.

1990 Mountain Bike Hall of Fame inductee Ned Overend, who has been at the top of his mountain biking game for more than 20 years, rides at the 1999 Big Bear World Cup in Big Bear, California.

*Unlike many of the early riders, who were downhillers first and foremost, Ned was all about lungs and climbing.*

When he retired at the end of the 1996 season, Overend hardly slowed down. His main bike sponsor, Specialized, retained him for research and development and as a spokesperson and coach of its mountain bike team. He also got involved with the cycling clothing company Bouré. And he didn't quit riding and racing. He simply switched focus to mountain bike triathlons and duathlons.

## John Tomac

Tomes, The Tome, Tomac Attack, or Johnny T. was one of the first mountain bikers to have that nebulous "it" factor. His riding, which was stunning and fast, enthralled the mountain bike world. A gifted bike handler and former top BMX racer, he burst onto the scene while still a teen in 1984. At 17, he won the National BMX Cruiser Class Championship. He then tried out the new sport of mountain bike racing.

Tomac was very good. He quickly learned how to train and race both up the hills and down, and he became a fierce competitor. While Tomac seemed to be a natural descender, he was also incredibly strong, winning a national criterium championship in 1988 on the road and climbing with the best road racers. He even tried racing as a professional road racer in Europe in 1990 and 1991 while racing

Inducted into the Mountain Bike Hall of Fame in 1991, John Tomac competes in the cross-country event at the 1994 World Cup Championship in Vail, Colorado. He also rode in the downhill events at the same event.

John Tomac at the 1997 World Cup Downhill in Mont-Sainte-Anne, Quebec, Canada.

John Tomac going all out at the 1999 Sea Otter Classic dual slalom event in Monterey, California.

as a professional mountain bike racer around the world.

Tomac won a mountain bike World Championship in Italy in 1991, his highest honor. But it obscures the fact that he remained competitive as both a cross-country and downhill rider throughout the 1990s, an era when the sport was becoming incredibly specialized. Amaz-

ingly, he closed out his career by focusing on downhill racing, winning the downhill nationals in 1997, a year after winning the cross-country natz. He retired from competition in 2000.

Once into retirement, Tomac also focused on designing bikes, which he does for the Tomac line of the American Bicycle Group.

## Juliana Furtado

Like a number of other mountain bike greats, Furtado was a crossover success. Before mountain bike racing, Furtado was a ski racer and a member of the national ski team from 1982–87 (she joined the team when she was 15). Her budding ski career was dashed by several knee operations, and she turned to cycling to get her competitive fix. Seemingly filled with anger, guilt, and a lack of confidence, she relished the pain of going all out on a bike. The faster she rode, the better she chased her demons.

Success on the bike came fast for Juliana, and her list of accomplishments is awesome. She won the National Road Championship in 1989, while still in college. She tried out mountain bike racing in 1990 and won the inaugural World Championships in Durango. She remained on top for the next six years, winning three World Cups, five national championships, even the Downhill World Championships in 1992. In 1993, she had a "perfect" season, winning every World Cup and NORBA National Race she entered, totaling a streak of 17 straight victories. She continued her winning ways through 1996, when she was selected to ride the first women's mountain bike race at the Atlanta Olympics.

Success eluded her in 1997, when she felt sick much of the year. At the end of the season, it was determined she was suffering from lupus, an autoimmune disorder, and she hung up her wheels.

Like many cyclists before her, she went into the bike industry. Furtado is currently a partner in Wylder, designing women-specific bikes and accessories.

*Success on the bike came fast for Furtado, and her list of accomplishments is awesome.*

Hall of Famer Juliana Furtado at the 1994 World Cup Championship Downhill in Vail, Colorado.

## Missy Giove

Like Juliana Furtado, Missy Giove came from New York and had a background in skiing. A hellion as a junior racer, she always seemed to be pushing the limits of speed, control, and behavior. She was as crazy off the bike as she was fast on it, and she was really fast. At the first World Championships in 1990, she won the junior division downhill event.

Juliana Furtado during the 1997 World Cup Cross-Country event in Napa, California.

Missy Giove at the 1994 World Cup Championship in Vail, Colorado, where she finished first in the downhill competition.

It was only the beginning. Giove's gung-ho attitude and incredible skill made her a media magnet. One of her classic quips meditating on her success was, "I guess I just have bigger ovaries." Tattoos, pierces, buzz-cut blonde sides and dreadlocks on top, a dead piranha around her neck as a good luck charm: She was perfect for the sport. Whether or not she sprinkled the ashes of her dead dog in her bra or wiped them on her forehead before a race has never been confirmed.

## *Missy Giove's gung-ho attitude and incredible skill made her a media magnet.*

Missy demonstrated that different was better. Sponsors flocked to her despite a radical image, temper tantrums, and being an open lesbian, something that is often treated like Kryptonite by large corporations.

She seems to ride in only two speeds: on the edge of control and out of control. She would often win, nabbing the World Championship in the downhill in 1994 as well as the Downhill World Cup in 1996 and 1997, but her crashes have been almost as spectacular as her victories. Crashing may have broken her bones (39 and counting), including stints in a wheelchair due to a broken pelvis, but it hasn't dampened her spirit or prevented her from tearing up any course she races down.

The Missile is also known for supporting causes she believes in, having donated her car and plenty of cash to struggling racers.

Missy Giove, whose extreme personality, skills, and accomplishments have made her a star on the women's circuit.

### Greg Herbold

Greg Herbold was the first-ever Downhill World Champion, winning in his hometown of Durango, Colorado, in 1990. Originally a cross-country racer, he found that downhilling favored his bike-handling skills. Combining those skills with an astute eye for equipment design made him a top racer. He was one of the first pros to embrace Rock Shox. H-Ball was always playing with his equipment, trying to get the most out of it. This attention landed him gigs as a technical adviser to Shimano and a number of other companies. In his retirement, he works for both Grip Shift and Rock Shox.

*Greg Herbold was the first-ever Downhill World Champion, winning in his hometown of Durango, Colorado in 1990.*

A goofy guy, good with a turn of phrase, he became known as a color commentator and a movie star. The latter is due to his appearances in cycling videos, most notably *Tread*, the first mountain bike movie. It has been said that he remains the most popular mountain bike racer in Japan.

### Paola Pezzo

La Pezzo raced into fame with her awesome ride at the 1996 Atlanta Olympics, where she became the first woman to win a gold medal at an Olympic mountain bike race. Not only did

*Opposite:* Greg Herbold at the 1994 World Cup Championship in Vail, Colorado. Herbold was inducted into the Mountain Bike Hall of Fame in 1996.

***Above and next page:*** Two-time Olympic gold medalist and Hall of Famer Paola Pezzo in Napa, California, during the 2001 season and racing at the Quebec World Cup at Mont-Sainte-Anne, Quebec, Canada, in 1997, where she placed first in cross-country.

*Pezzo was able to parlay both her mountain bike skills and sex appeal into an unforgettable career.*

91

she solo for the win, but she did it in fine style, wearing an unforgettable Italian national team skinsuit with silver shorts and the top almost totally unzipped.

Pezzo was able to parlay both her mountain bike skills and sex appeal into an unforgettable career. She was the star of many ad campaigns, once posing as Little Red Riding Hood. Gold lamé cycling shorts with a team jersey was her preferred look. She won both the 1997 Mountain Bike World Championships and the World Cup, and was a perennial favorite through her victory at the 2000 Olympics. She retired in 2001.

## Hans Rey

Once a trick rider, always a trick rider. No Way Rey came from the world of observed trials, where he was a master. GT Bicycles sponsored him, and he raced the international mountain bike circuit, doing trials, trick rides, as well as timed gravity events. As a trials rider, he was Germany's trials champ from 1982–85, Switzerland's champion from 1984–86, and U.S. champion from 1987–91. Hans won the World Championship in trials in 1990, 1992, and 1993. He also did dual slalom, an event where he won a bronze medal at the 1993 World Championship.

Extreme mountain biker and Hall of Famer Hans Rey performs in Vail, Colorado.

Always a hit no matter where in the world he performs, Hans Rey exhibits his skills here in Big Bear, California.

Shots of him riding in exotic places, like Machu Picchu and Hawaii, were made into photo features in cycling mags.

Leaving competition behind, Rey formed the Hans Rey Adventure Team. The team is a sponsored endeavor that rides in beautiful places and performs impressive feats. Both adventure photographers and racing cyclists are included on the squad.

## *Hans won the World Championship in trials in 1990, 1992, and 1993.*

### The Stuff of Legends

Remember, this is only a short list, one that includes a brief cross-section of some of mountain biking's most famous pioneers in a number of different ways.

Whether you prefer the "crazy" outgoing nature of downhillers, the soulful visions of cross-country rides and its riders, or the general enthusiasm of this magnificent sport that crosses generations and personalities, mountain biking today has a long list of influential characters.

The high-profile riders are the most visible, yet the inventors and innovators have enabled them through the years to go faster, farther, and higher. Writers and photographers have their place, too, as do bike mechanics and sponsors. The list goes on. What has most created a spot of reverence for mountain biking within American and worldwide culture is you and all of the other colorful riders out there, those of us who ride on each and every day and even into the night.

Rey continued to rack up trials victories through 1997, but by then he was already a star of stage and screen. His trick riding was featured during the closing ceremonies of the 1996 Atlanta Olympics. He had been cast as one of the cyclists in *Tread,* and had been featured in many television shows, including the first drama starring bike cops, *Pacific Blue.*

In addition to his work in front of movie cameras, he is also a star of still photographs.

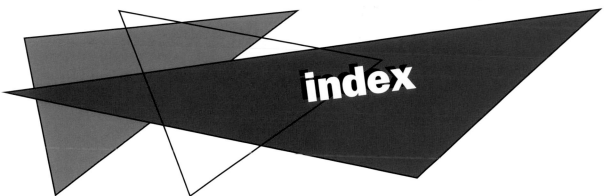

# index

**95**

**Complete Bike Maintenance**
ISBN 0-7603-1330-X

**The American Bicycle**
ISBN 0-7603-1045-9

**Schwinn Bicycles**
ISBN 0-7603-1298-2

**The Bicycle Repair Book**
ISBN 0-933201-55-9

**Road Bike Maintenance**
ISBN 0-933201-79-6

**Mountain Bike Maintenance**
ISBN 0-933201-65-6

**Schwinn**
ISBN 1-58068-003-8

**Classic American Bicycles**
ISBN 1-58068-001-1

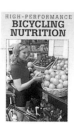

**High-Performance
Bicycling Nutrition**
ISBN 0-933201-92-3